Go, Critter, Go!

Flash, Firefly, Flash!

Dana Meachen Rau

Marshall Cavendish
Benchmark
New York

Fireflies are black.

Fireflies are orange.

Fireflies have four wings.

Fireflies fly in the dark.

Fireflies fly over grass.

Fireflies have little lights.

Fireflies flash their lights.

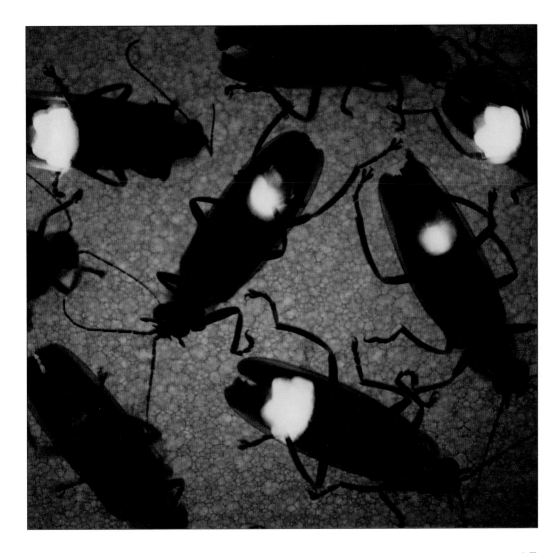

15

Fireflies flash to more fireflies.

Flash, firefly, flash!

Words We Know

black

dark

grass

light

orange

wings

Index

Page numbers in **boldface** are illustrations.

About the Author

Dana Meachen Rau is an author, editor, and illustrator. A graduate of Trinity College in Hartford, Connecticut, she has written more than one hundred fifty books for children, including nonfiction, biographies, early readers, and historical fiction. She lives with her family in Burlington, Connecticut.

With thanks to the Reading Consultants:

Nanci Vargus, Ed.D., is an Assistant Professor of Elementary Education at the University of Indianapolis.

Beth Walker Gambro received her M.S. Ed. Reading from the University of St. Francis, Joliet, Illinois.

Marshall Cavendish
99 White Plains Road
Tarrytown, New York 10591-9001
www.marshallcavendish.us

Library of Congress Cataloging-in-Publication Data

Rau, Dana Meachen, 1971–
Flash, firefly, flash! / by Dana Meachen Rau.
    p. cm. — (Bookworms. Go, critter, go!)
Summary: "Describes characteristics and behaviors of fireflies"—Provided by publisher.
Includes index.
ISBN 978-0-7614-3263-0 (PB)
ISBN 978-0-7614-2651-6 (HB)
1. Fireflies—Juvenile literature. I. Title. II. Series.
QL596.L28R38 2007
595.76'44—dc22
2006034094

Editor: Christina Gardeski
Publisher: Michelle Bisson
Designer: Virginia Pope
Art Director: Anahid Hamparian

Photo Research by Anne Burns Images

Cover Photo by *Photo Researchers*/Darwin Dale

The photographs in this book are used with permission and through the courtesy of:
Visuals Unlimited: pp. 1, 13, 15, 21TL Jeff Daly. *Animals Animals*: pp. 3, 5, 9, 20TL&TR,
21TR James E. Lloyd; pp. 11, 20B E.R. Degginger. *Jupiter Images*: pp. 7, 21B Paulo De Oliveira.
Photo Researchers: p. 17 Keith Kent; p. 19 E.R. Degginger.

Printed in Malaysia
1   3   5   6   4   2